HOW TO HANDLE EMOTIONS FOR KIDS

"TEACHING KIDS TO MANAGE AND EXPRESS THEIR FEELINGS"

JACOB S. KING

This book is intended to help provide parents and caregivers with information about how to handle emotions for kids. The information is provided for educational and entertainment purposes only and is not intended to replace any professional medical advice. The reader should consult with a qualified professional before taking any action based on the information provided in this book. The author and publisher are not responsible for any specific damages or negative consequences from any, action, application or preparation, to any person reading or following the information in this book.

If you like this book, please leave a positive review on Amazon. I would appreciate it.
Thanks.

TABLE OF CONTENTS

PART I

INTRODUCTION

Having strong emotions is a normal part of life for children, but it can be difficult for them to handle those emotions in healthy ways. It's important to teach kids how to recognize, understand, and express their emotions in a healthy way. This can help them to form positive relationships, develop a strong sense of self-esteem, and make good decisions in the future.

Welcome to **How to Handle Emotions for Kids**! This book is designed to help parents and other caregivers understand and manage the emotions of young children in a positive and constructive way. We will explore how to recognize and respond to children's emotions, how to encourage healthy emotional expression, and how to help children build emotional resilience.

We know that it can be challenging to figure out how to deal with children's emotions. Children are still learning how to make sense of their experiences and express their feelings in a healthy way. As adults, we can provide guidance and support to help our children navigate their emotions and develop healthy coping strategies.

In this guide, we'll explore ways to help your child learn how to handle their emotions, we will also explore a variety of strategies and techniques that can be used to help children learn how to manage their emotions. From practical tips for handling tantrums to games and activities for building emotional intelligence, this book is full of ideas and resources to help you and your child. Understanding your Child's emotion is the key to guiding them through life.

Some tips that will be covered include:
• Recognizing and understanding emotions
• Setting healthy boundaries
• Coping strategies
• Communicating feelings
• Developing emotional intelligence

By the end of this guide, your child will have the tools they need to manage their emotions in a positive and productive way. We hope that this book will help you to understand and respond to your child's emotions in a way that encourages healthy emotional development. Thank you for taking the time to read this book and for investing in your child's emotional wellbeing.

We are happy to provide this book to help you understand and learn how to handle emotions for kids.

Good luck and enjoy your journey!

PART II
RECOGNIZING UNDERSTANDING EMOTIONS

Recognizing your emotions

If you ever find yourself feeling confused or overwhelmed, recognizing your emotions can help you understand why you feel the way you do. Learning to recognize your emotions is an important part of growing up.

When you can recognize your emotions, you can learn how to express them in a healthy way. Being able to recognize and express your emotions can help you build stronger relationships with other people and better manage difficult situations.

One way to start recognizing your emotions is to pay attention to how your body feels. What do you notice? Do you feel warm or hot? Is your heart racing? Are your palms sweaty? Are your muscles tense? Does your stomach feel queasy? All of these physical sensations can help you understand how you're feeling.

Another way to recognize emotions is to pay attention to your thoughts. What are you thinking about? Are you worrying or feeling anxious? Are you feeling excited or hopeful? Maybe you're feeling frustrated or angry. All of these thoughts can help you understand how you're feeling.

It can be helpful to pay attention to the types of behaviors you engage in. Are you avoiding certain people or activities? Do you notice yourself zoning out or having difficulty concentrating? Are you having difficulty sleeping or eating? All of these behaviors can help you recognize your emotions.

Once you can identify your emotions, you can make a plan for how to manage them. Maybe you need to take a break, talk to a friend, or get some fresh air. However, you decide to manage your emotions, it's important to remember that it's okay to feel whatever you feel. With practice, you can become more aware of your emotions and learn how to express them in a healthy way.

Recognizing kids Emotions

It's important to help kids learn how to recognize and express their emotions. When kids can identify and name their emotions, they are better able to understand and accept them. Knowing how to handle emotions can help children become resilient and cope better with life's challenges.

Start by talking about emotions. Talk about what different emotions look like, sound like, and feel like. Discuss different scenarios that can lead to different emotions. Explain that it's normal to feel a range of emotions throughout the day, and that it's ok to express these feelings.

Help kids find words to describe their feelings. Encourage them to use "feeling words" such as happy, sad, angry, scared, frustrated, excited, and proud. Make sure they know it's ok to have all kinds of feelings, and that it's ok to express them.

Encourage kids find healthy ways of expressing their emotions. Show them how to take deep breaths when they are feeling angry or frustrated, or how to express their feelings through artwork or music. Talk to them about how to handle difficult emotions in appropriate ways.

Encourage your kids to talk about their emotions. Ask them questions like "How do you feel right now?" Or "What do you think caused that emotion?" pay critical attention to their answers and give validation to their feelings. Remind them that their feelings are important and should be taken seriously.

Finally, remember that it's ok to make mistakes. Kids are still learning how to recognize and express their emotions, and it can take time to get it right. Offer support and understanding, and provide them with opportunities to practice. With time and practice, they will learn to recognize and express their emotions in healthy ways.

Understanding your emotions

In life, it is absolutely natural and normal for feel emotions. Everyone experiences different emotions, and it's important to take the time to understand what those emotions mean and how to process them.

When an emotion is strong, it can be hard to cope with at first. That's why it's important to take a few moments to pause and take a deep breath. This will help you to calm down and begin to process the emotion.

When we don't understand how we feel, it can be helpful to talk with someone. A parent, teacher, or trusted friend can be a great listener to help you figure out what you're feeling. Talking can help you to recognize and understand your emotions.

It's also important to remember that some emotions are not bad. It is also normal as human to feel angry, sad, or scared. All of these emotions help us to understand ourselves and the world around us.

When it comes to understanding emotions, it's important to be kind to yourself. Take a few moments each day to check in with yourself and your emotions. This will help you to figure out what you're feeling and how to best manage it. With a little practice, you'll be able to better understand your emotions and use them to help you make better decisions.

Understanding kids' emotions
Children are rapidly growing and developing, learning more about the world around them and how to express themselves. As children learn to understand and express their emotions, it can be a difficult and often overwhelming process. It is important for adults to be patient and understanding when children express their emotions.

When children become upset, they may not be able to express how they are feeling in words. It is important to help them identify the emotion they are feeling and talk through it with them. It is also important to be empathetic when children express their emotions.

When a child is feeling overwhelmed, take the time to listen to them and validate their feelings. Ask open-ended questions about why they are feeling a certain way, and help them find ways to express their emotions without resorting to physical aggression.

It is important to help children understand that it is okay to feel emotions, and to help them learn how to manage their emotions. Model healthy ways to cope with emotions, such as taking deep breaths, counting to ten, or talking to a trusted adult.

Teaching children how to understand and express their emotions is an important part of their development. With patience, understanding, and guidance, children can learn to recognize, express, and manage their emotions.

PART III

TEACHING KIDS HOW TO RECOGNIZE
AND EXPRESS THEIR EMOTIONAL STATE

Teaching kids to identify and express their feelings is an important skill for children to develop. Knowing how to recognize and express feelings helps children to understand their own emotions and those of others, which can help them to build strong relationships and make better decisions. Teaching kids to identify and express their feelings can also help them to cope with stress and anxiety in a healthy way. Learning how to recognize and express emotions is an essential skill that can help kids throughout their lives.

By providing children with opportunities to practice this skill and offering support when they experience strong emotions, parents and caregivers can help children to become more self-aware and resilient. Teaching kids to identify and express their feelings can help them to build confidence, strengthen relationships, and lead healthier lives.

This article will provide an overview of how to teach kids to identify and express their feelings, as well as tips and strategies for supporting children as they learn.

By these tips below, you can help your child learn to identify and express their feelings in a healthy and productive way:

1. **Model Emotional Awareness:** It's important for kids to learn that it's okay to express their feelings. Parents and caregivers can model this behavior by being open and honest about their own feelings.

2. **Talk About Feelings:** When kids are feeling a certain way, take the time to talk about it. Try to know how they're feeling and why they are feeling so.

3. **Read Books About Feelings:** Reading books about emotions can help kids learn to recognize and express their feelings.

4. **Play Games:** Games are a great way to help kids practice identifying and expressing their feelings. For example, have them match the emotion with the facial expression.

5. **Have an Open Dialogue:** Encourage kids to talk about their feelings and listen without judgment. This will help them feel more comfortable expressing themselves.

6. **Acknowledge Feelings:** It's important to recognize and acknowledge a child's feelings, even if you don't agree with them. This will help to have a sense of belonging.

7. **Be Understanding:** Be patient with children as they learn to identify and express their

feelings. Remember that it can be a difficult process for them.

8. **Encourage Positive Coping Strategies:** Help kids find positive ways to cope with their feelings, such as writing, drawing, or talking.

9. **Provide Support:** Let kids know that you are there to support them and that you are available to listen

10. **Praise Efforts:** Praise children when they identify and express their feelings in an appropriate manner. This will inspire them to continue to do so.

In conclusion, teaching kids to identify and express their feelings is an important part of helping them become emotionally healthy adults. By doing so, they are given the tools to develop healthy relationships and cope with difficult emotions.

Parents, teachers, and other caregivers should work together to create a safe and supportive environment where children feel comfortable sharing their feelings. Through activities, discussion, and modeling, children can learn how to recognize and express their feelings in a healthy and appropriate way.

Setting Healthy Boundaries

Setting healthy boundaries for kids' emotions means helping them to identify and manage their emotions in a healthy way. This can involve teaching them to recognize and label their feelings, expressing their feelings in appropriate ways, understanding how their emotions affect their behavior, and learning to take responsibility for their actions. It also involves setting limits and providing consequences for inappropriate behaviors. As part of setting healthy boundaries for kids' emotions, parents and caregivers should also provide support and understanding, and create an environment that encourages and rewards positive emotions.

It is important for parents and caregivers to set boundaries for kids' emotions to help them learn to manage their own emotions and gain self-control. This helps to ensure that children are able to develop emotionally, socially, and cognitively in a healthy and safe way. Setting boundaries for kids' emotions also teaches them how to effectively communicate their feelings, express themselves, and develop healthy relationships with others.

PART IV

HELPING KIDS DEVELOP SELF-REGULATION SKILLS

Self-regulation is a key skill for children to develop in order to lead healthy and successful lives. It is the ability to effectively manage and control one's emotions, thoughts, and behaviors in order to make positive choices. Self-regulation skills are important for children to learn as they help them develop better problem-solving skills, make better decisions, and build healthier relationships. As parents, teachers, and caregivers, we can help children develop these important skills. By providing a safe and supportive environment, engaging in activities that promote self-regulation, and modeling appropriate self-regulation behaviors, we can help children develop the important skills they need to be successful.

Self-regulation skills are essential for children to develop as they grow and mature. By providing a safe and supportive environment, engaging in activities that promote self-regulation, and modeling appropriate self-regulation behaviors, we can help our children develop the important skills they need to be successful. These tips below, can help them develop strong self-regulation skills:

1. **Model and encourage self-regulation:** Demonstrate the importance of self-regulation by setting an example and speaking positively about it. Praise children when they display self-regulatory behavior.

2. **Teach problem-solving skills:** Help children identify possible solutions to their problems and encourage them to think of alternatives. Model problem-solving and provide support as needed.

3. **Practice self-talk:** Teach children to talk to themselves in a positive way. Help them recognize the power of their own words and the importance of being kind to themselves.

4. **Help children recognize their emotions:**
   Talk to children about their feelings and help
   them identify the physical sensations
   associated with their emotions. Point out how
   certain behaviors can help or hinder their
   ability to manage their emotions.

5. **Create a safe space:** Establish a calm and
   supportive environment in which children
   feel safe to express their emotions and take
   risks.

6. **Encourage positive coping strategies:** Help
   children develop positive coping strategies
   such as deep breathing, journaling, or
   drawing.

7. **Set limits:** Establish clear limits and
   expectations for behavior. Make sure that
   children understand the consequences for
   breaking the rules.

8. **Encourage physical activity:** Physical activity can help children manage their emotions and feel more in control. Encourage children to engage in physical activities that they enjoy.

9. **Take breaks:** Teach children to take breaks when they are feeling overwhelmed. Encourage them to find a quiet space to relax and regroup.

10. **Cultivate a growth mindset:** Help children understand that they can learn and grow from mistakes. Encourage them to view challenges as opportunities for growth.

11. **Show patience and understanding:** Children need time to learn and practice self-regulation skills. Showing patience and understanding will help them feel safe and supported as they work on these skills.

12. **Model healthy behaviors:** Children learn from what they see and observe. Modeling self-regulation skills such as taking deep breaths, counting to 10, or using positive self-talk will help them learn how to do the same.

13. **Provide structure and routines:** Establishing a daily routine and providing structure will help children learn how to regulate their behavior.

14. **Give choices:** Give children choices when possible so they can practice making decisions.

15. **Encourage problem-solving:** Help children practice problem-solving by guiding them through difficult situations.

16. **Promote self-awareness:** Helping children become aware of their emotions, thoughts,

and behaviors will help them build self-regulation skills.

17. **Praise and reward positive behaviors:** Celebrate successes and reward positive behaviors to encourage children to continue practicing self-regulation skills.

By incorporating these tips into your parenting or caregiving style, you can help foster children's self-regulation skills. With practice, patience, and guidance, children can learn the skills they need to lead healthy and successful lives.

Communicating Feelings

Communicating feelings is the process of expressing and understanding emotions. It is important for children to learn how to recognize and express their feelings in order to develop healthy relationships. It can help them build self-esteem and self-confidence. Kids can communicate their feelings in different ways, such as talking, drawing, playing, or writing.

The most important thing is to listen to them and show empathy and understanding. It is also important to model healthy communication skills and provide guidance when needed.

It is important to acknowledge and validate the feelings of children. This means recognizing and understanding their emotions without judging or discounting them. By doing this, children can learn to trust their feelings and express them in a safe and healthy way.

When communicating feelings, it is important to be patient, understanding, and supportive. It is also important to provide a safe and supportive environment for children to express their feelings. Encourage them to take time to talk about their feelings and give them opportunities to practice communication skills. Finally, provide comfort and reassurance when needed.

PART V

DEALING WITH DIFFICULT EMOTIONS

Dealing with difficult emotions can be challenging, but it is important to take time to process these feelings. Start by recognizing and acknowledging the emotions you are feeling. This can help you better understand them and create insight into what is causing them. Once you have identified the emotions, it is helpful to practice self-care. This can include activities such as taking a walk, talking to a friend, or journaling. Additionally, it may be helpful to practice calming techniques such as deep breathing, progressive muscle relaxation, or meditation. Finally, it is important to talk to a mental health professional if the emotions become too overwhelming.

By taking the time to recognize and process difficult emotions, you can create a healthier and happier environment for yourself.

On the other hand, in the process of parenting, dealing with kids' difficult emotions can be challenging, but it doesn't have to be overwhelming. The key is to remember that emotions are normal, and that it's OK to feel them. Even if the emotions are strong or uncomfortable, it's important to remember that they are a part of life.

Start by validating the emotions. Let your child know that it's OK to feel whatever they're feeling, and that it's normal to have difficult emotions. Acknowledge their emotions without judgement, and provide them with support.

Help your child to identify and name their emotions. Ask them to describe what they're feeling, and help them to put a name to it. This can help them to gain a better understanding of their emotions and to better process them.

Once they've identified their emotions, help them to find healthy ways to express and cope with them.

This could include talking about the emotion, writing it down, engaging in a physical activity, or playing music.

Most important, to be patient and understanding is very vital. Difficult emotions can be overwhelming, and it can take time for your child to learn how to manage them.

By providing your child with the necessary support and understanding, you can help them to better understand and cope with their emotions.

Here are some tips to guide you through dealing with difficult emotions for your kids:

1. **Talk about it:** Talking to a parent, teacher, or another trusted adult can help kids sort out and make sense of their difficult emotions.

2. **Take a break:** Give your child a chance to take a break from whatever is causing the

difficult emotion. This could be playing a game, going for a walk, or listening to music.

3. **Express yourself:** Help your child find a healthy way to express their emotions. This could be through drawing, writing, or playing an instrument.

4. **Get moving:** Exercise is a great way to help your child work through difficult emotions. Going for a run, playing a sport, or having a dance party can all be effective.

5. **Practice mindfulness:** Teach your child to practice mindful breathing, which can help them feel more grounded and relaxed in difficult moments.

6. **Reach out for help:** If your child is struggling with difficult emotions, it's important to seek help from a mental health

professional. This could either be a therapist, psychologist, or psychiatrist.

7. **Connect with nature:** Being in nature can be very calming and soothing. Take a walk in the park or go to the beach together.

8. **Practice self-care:** Encourage your child to practice self-care activities like taking a bubble bath, reading a book, or doing a fun art project.

9. **Stay positive:** Help your child focus on the positive things in their life and appreciate the good moments. This can help them get through tough times.

10. **Get enough sleep:** Sleep is essential for emotional wellbeing. Ensure that your child is getting adequate sleep especially at night.

11. **Reach out to others:** Encourage your child to reach out to friends and family for support. This can help them feel less alone in difficult moments.

It is essential to helping kids learn how to manage their emotions in a healthy way. Having an open and honest dialogue, setting firm boundaries and expectations, providing emotional support, and using positive reinforcement are all key elements of successfully managing children's emotional expressions. Additionally, encouraging children to express their feelings and providing them with the right tools to do so can help them learn to manage their emotions better. Ultimately, helping children understand and express their emotions can provide them with lifelong skills to better deal with their own emotions in the future.

PART VI

BUILDING EMOTIONAL RESILIENCE

Building kids emotional resilience is an important part of parenting. It involves helping kids learn to identify, understand, and manage their emotions in a healthy way. It is important to help kids learn how to cope with stress and difficult situations, and how to bounce back from setbacks. Building emotional resilience also helps kids develop skills like problem-solving, communication, and self-regulation. By helping kids develop these skills, they can become more confident and better prepared to handle life's challenges.

Some activities and strategies that can help build kids emotional resilience include teaching them how to identify and express their feelings, helping them practice problem-solving skills, discussing challenges with them and offering positive reinforcement and encouragement. It is also important to provide a supportive environment where kids feel safe to express their emotions and be heard.

By helping kids build emotional resilience, parents can provide them with a strong foundation for lifelong success and happiness.

Emotional resilience refers to the ability to bounce back from challenging situations and difficult emotions. It can help kids develop the skills to handle difficult emotions, cope with stress, and take on life challenges with confidence.

Here are some tips to help build emotional resilience in kids:

1. Teach kids how to be mindful and self-compassionate. Mindfulness and self-compassion can help kids recognize and regulate their emotions so they can respond rather than react to difficult situations.

2. Help kids manage stress by teaching them healthy coping skills. Teach them to take deep breaths, practice positive self-talk, and focus on the things they can control.

3. Encourage kids to build self-esteem. Self-esteem is key to developing emotional resilience. Help kids become aware of their strengths and accomplishments and show them that mistakes are an opportunity to learn and grow.

4. Model how to express emotions in healthy ways. Kids learn how to process and express their emotions by watching the adults in their lives. Show them how to express their feelings in healthy, productive ways.

5. Help kids develop problem-solving skills. Teaching kids to identify the problem, brainstorm solutions, and find the best

solution can help them become more resilient in the face of challenges.

6. Encourage kids to be resilient. Show kids that they can handle difficult situations and emotions by praising them for their efforts and resilience.

It's important to give kids the tools to recognize, express, and process their emotions, as well as develop problem-solving skills, strong relationships, and healthy coping mechanisms. By equipping kids with the skills to handle difficult emotions and build resilience, they can develop the emotional strength to face life's challenges and achieve success. By helping kids develop emotional resilience, we are setting them up for success and helping them to become resilient, confident adults.

Developing emotional intelligence

Developing emotional intelligence for kids involves helping children become more aware of their emotions, as well as the emotions of others. It involves teaching children how to manage their emotions in healthy ways, such as being able to recognize and express their feelings, taking responsibility for their own emotions, and learning how to empathize with others. It also involves teaching them problem-solving skills and how to build positive relationships. In essence, developing emotional intelligence for kids helps them better understand themselves and others, and to effectively manage their own emotions.

This can be done in a variety of ways, including teaching relaxation techniques and mindfulness, role-playing scenarios to help them practice managing their emotions, and providing positive reinforcement when they handle their emotions in appropriate ways. Parents can also model how to express and manage emotions in healthy ways, and provide an emotionally safe environment where they can talk about their feelings and be heard.

PART VII
CLOSING THOUGHTS

Handling difficult emotions in children is a challenge that all parents face. However, with patience, understanding, and the right tools, it is possible to help children learn to manage and express their feelings in a healthy way. Teaching children positive coping skills, such as deep breathing and positive self-talk, can help them manage their emotions in a more constructive way. It is also important to validate their feelings and provide them with a safe space to express their feelings without fear of judgement. Setting boundaries and providing clear expectations can also help children learn to manage their emotions and make better choices.

In conclusion, this book has provided parent, caregivers and even children with the necessary tools to understand, recognize, and manage their emotions. It has discussed some of the common emotions that children experience, how they can be expressed in healthy ways, and how to create a positive environment to help them be their best selves. It has also provided helpful tips on how to talk to children about their feelings and how to handle difficult situations. With the knowledge and tools provided, children can learn to handle their emotions in a healthy way and become more confident and resilient.

Overall, this book has been a great guide for helping parent, caregivers and children to understand and manage their emotions. It has provided them with a wealth of information on how to deal with different emotions, how to express them in healthy ways, and how to create an environment that encourages emotional growth. Hopefully, this book has been able to help children better understand and manage their feelings and help them to become more emotionally mature and resilient.

Finally, modeling healthy emotional expression and providing consistent, loving support can help children learn to recognize and express their emotions in a healthy way. With these tools, parents can help their children develop the skills to handle difficult emotions in a healthy and productive way.

Thank you for reading this book. If you find this book helpful, please leave a positive review on Amazon. I would appreciate it.
Thanks.

www.ingramcontent.com/pod-product-compliance
Lightning Source LLC
Chambersburg PA
CBHW060923130726
48001CB00006B/2379